HIP HOP RAISED ME, JESUS SAVED ME

THE MAKING OF AN APOSTLE

Richard Scotman

Hip Hop Raised Me, Jesus Saved Me
Copyright © 2023 Richard Scotman

This book is not intended as a substitute for the medical advice of physicians. The reader should regularly consult a physician in matters relating to their health and particularly with respect to any symptoms that may require diagnosis or medical attention.

ISBN

Printed in USA by 48HrBooks (www.48HrBooks.com)

TABLE OF CONTENTS

CHAPTER 1 1
GROWING UP IN NEW YORK

CHAPTER 2 11
HIGH SCHOOL AND HIP HOP

CHAPTER 3 19
MY INTRODUCTION TO THE PARTY LIFE

CHAPTER 4 29
FAMILY TIME

CHAPTER 5 37
THE DEVIL'S PLAN DIDN'T WORK

CHAPTER 6 41
TIME TO MAN UP

CHAPTER 7 47
MY DOWNWARD SPIRAL

CHAPTER 8 63
SALVATION GRACE COMES TO MY FAMILY

CHAPTER 9 69
WALKING WITH JESUS

CHAPTER 10 77
CALLED TO GREATNESS

CHAPTER 1
GROWING UP IN NEW YORK

Jeremiah 1:5 "Before I formed thee in the belly, I knew thee; and before thou camest forth out of the womb I sanctified thee, and I ordained thee a prophet unto the nations."

This journey through my life I hope will help you to come to the saving knowledge of Jesus Christ. We all have a purpose in why we were put on this earth. Our life circumstances, no matter how difficult, are a part of the process to get us to become who God has called us to be. I have heard it said that; the greater your calling is, the greater your trials are. After many ups and downs and trials in my life. I am now a humble servant of Almighty God. Serving him as a son, a husband, a father, and an Apostle. It is by God's grace alone that I can function in all these different roles. On my own I can do nothing and without Jesus Christ, I am nothing. This is my story:

My name is Richard Mark Scotman and I was born to Anthony and Beverly Scotman on June 29, 1978 at Jamaica Hospital in Jamaica, Queens NY. I didn't find this out until recently, but on that day, when my mother went to the hospital. She was rushed into surgery to have an emergency c-section because of some complications with me in her womb. I could have died that day but thank God that he had a plan for my life and kept me alive.

My parents had just gotten married the year before and were living in a small apartment in Forest Hills, Queens NY.

My dad was a computer engineer and was working for a big company making good money. Now that they had started a family and had the money, my parents decided to buy their first home together in Elmont, NY. Soon after our move into this new home, my brother Jason was born. Four years later my parents had their third son, named Gordon. My mother was really trying for a little girl, but God had other plans. So, I became the oldest of three boys between my parents and I was raised in Long Island, NY.

My parents were Catholics so growing up we did the typical Catholic religious routine. My brothers and I were baptized as infants with our "godparents" there. Then we did communion and confirmation as we got older. We went to mass on Sundays, but my parents were not born again and did not have a real relationship with Jesus Christ. I never remember ever hearing my parents talk about God outside of going to church. As a matter of fact, I never saw them reading the Bible or even praying other than occasionally thanking God for a meal.

As I came to find out later, this is the life of many people in the Catholic Church. Some do actually know the Lord, read the Bible, and have a personal relationship with him but others don't. When I actually started reading the Bible, there were no Popes, Nuns, Holy water, rosary beads, baptism of infants, praying to Mary, and no confessional booths in there. So where did all of this come from? I found out that they were made up by men and most of these things actually go against the teachings of the Bible, which is God's word. Sadly, many of my friends and family were following these ways but God is waking people up to the truth.

My parents were both born and raised on the island of Jamaica and grew up Catholic, so they did not know any better. They came to America to go to college and to make a better life for themselves. They were one of the millions of immigrants who come to this country to chase the American dream. My parents met each other in their mid-20's. My dad had been married before and had a son and a daughter both of whom have different mothers. My dad was a ladies man and always had a way with women. My mother was a beautiful and innocent bookworm type who was studying to be a lawyer. Their relationship was the typical good girl falls for, not so good guy situation that you see in movies. This would later have a major effect on my life as you will see.

My brother Jason and I were very close in our younger years in Elmont and life was good for us. I can remember us out in front of our house after big snowstorms. We would make snowmen and have snowball fights with other children in the neighborhood. He was 2 years younger than me and I loved having a brother to play with.

Everything seemed great when we were younger, but as I got a little older, I started to notice that my parents would argue a lot. Especially late at night because that's when my dad usually got home. We didn't understand why, but it became a normal thing for us. As the years went by, the less we saw our dad because he was always working and going on business trips. Therefore, my mother took care of us most of the time. My dad was there financially to pay the bills of course, but physically he was not around that much.

I love my dad and everything, but he wasn't there for my brothers and I as much as I would have wanted him to be when we were growing up. It really wasn't his fault. He wasn't a spiritual man and didn't understand what the enemy, the devil, was doing to our family. He did the best that he could with what he believed was the right way to raise his children. I appreciate everything my dad did because there are many men out there who totally abandon their children. So, I am grateful that my dad was in my life. As you will see God had a purpose and a plan in all that I went through with him anyway.

When my mother finished law school, she started working at a law firm in Manhattan. She would have to travel by train into the city every day which became very stressful for her. Especially when she had to leave her job to come get us from school early. Eventually she decided to open her own law practice. She was a great mom and wanted to be closer to home. This gave her the ability to have more freedom to take care of us. She had been making good money and her income now combined with my dad's was pretty heavy. They ended up buying a building on Francis Lewis Blvd in Queens. It was a great location for her to start her law practice and she quickly started getting business.

My parents were also able to move us into a bigger brand-new construction home in West Hempstead, NY. Not only were they making big money, but they started spending big too. It was a new five-bedroom two-and-a-half-bathroom home. It was right on the border of Garden City, which was one of the most affluent cities in Nassau County. My youngest brother Gordon was born in this home and we had plenty of room to play. Now that my mother had this new law practice, she ended up working long hours. She eventually had to hire a live-in babysitter to help her to take care of us.

We were the only black family in this brand-new community when we moved in. We were also one of the few black families in West Hempstead which was pretty awkward for us. Elmont was a more mixed city with a lot of minorities and my parents had friends there. Now we were in a predominantly white community, and we came to find out about this thing called racism. The elementary school that we went to was named George Washington elementary and we were one of two black families there. Being the only black boys in the school, my brother and I used to get picked on. It was a very uncomfortable experience for us, moving to a city like this.

I remember being bullied by one of the biggest children in the school named Carl. This went on for quite some time until one day. He called me out and wanted to fight me after school. I agreed to it because I was tired of being picked on. It wasn't like you see on TV where the whole school watched, but it was a classic bully gets beat up moment.

Lol…. As I was whipping Carl's butt his mother saw us fighting and came over to try to stop me and save her son. She actually tried to reprimand me and then her and my babysitter at the time, Erin almost started fighting each other. It was one of the most memorable times of my youth.

Unfortunately, while things got better for me at school, things started to go downhill for my brother Jason. I think the fact that my parents were always working caused my brother to feel neglected. He was the type of child who needed a lot of attention and care from his parents. He started lashing out at home and at school. He started getting bad grades and into problems with his teachers.

Matthew 6:24 "No man can serve two masters: for either he will hate the one, and love the other; or else he will hold to the one, and despise the other. Ye cannot serve God and mammon."

As I look back, I know that it was because of all the sin that my parents were in. They did not know that the life they were living caused all kinds of demons to come into our home. My dad would go out of town on business trips a lot. I learned later that he was cheating on my mother with different women, some in other states. My mother became a shopaholic I believe because of my dad's absence. After work, a lot of times she would go to different stores buying fancy clothes, jewelry, and all kinds of things for the house. They lived a very worldly or as the Bible would call it, carnal life. Loving money and what it could buy them. Mercedes

Benz became the car of choice for my parents and ironically my mother's middle name is Mercedes.

I remember when I was around thirteen or fourteen years old, my dad bought a Porsche. My childhood friend, Andrew and I used to sneak it out of the garage in the middle of the night and drive it around town. Thank God we never got caught! Who knows what he would have done, but this is kind of how I learned to drive stick shift. The clutch kept getting messed up, but my dad never found out that we were the reason why.

1 Timothy 6:10 "For the love of money is the root of all evil."

Not all but most of my parent's friends lived worldly as well so there weren't really any Godly influences around us. Everything was about chasing the almighty dollar. All they told us was to get good grades, so that we could go to a great college, and get a great job making a lot of money. All of this just so we could buy a nice house and have nice things. They never realized that without having God as your foundation, all these things meant nothing and could never satisfy them. I don't blame them for what they taught us because that's just the way most people think.

As a result, over the years things became worse and worse in our house. Jason was really acting up in school being disrespectful to his teachers. He would get suspended from school a lot and he started to become a bad influence on Gordon who was the youngest of the three of us. As the older brother I usually just kept to myself. Sometimes when Jason and I were around each other for too long we would end up fighting. It seemed like the older we got, the more we fought.

Eventually my mom and dad decided to take us out of the public-school system and put us in private schools. When it came to school, they were very strict and like I said they wanted us to get good grades. The problem was we were very much influenced by the TV and the music we listened to because our parents were always working. We started listening to hip hop and rap music. This was back in the late 80s and early 90s when hip hop and rap music were starting to explode. My parents thought it was the public school that was corrupting us, but it was really the music and the television. We were being raised by the culture that surrounded us and we thought it was cool.

When my dad was not away on a business trip, one of us was always getting in trouble with him and whipped for something. It was either we were getting bad grades in school or one of us was being disobedient to my mother. My dad was the one who did the disciplining in our home. We were usually whipped with a belt but sometimes we would get hit with a shoe or whatever he could grab at the time. When my mother tried to beat us, we would just laugh at her. We were really only scared of our dad and my mother knew this. All she had to say to us was; I'm going to tell your dad when he gets home, and we would be afraid. Sometimes I would start crying just because I knew a beating was coming. It was usually when I got a bad grade on a test or something.

A bad grade for us was anything less than a B-. They were trying to get us to be straight A students, but I ended up being more like a B/C student.

When I look back, the only good times I remember spending with my dad were when we went to play soccer games or went on family vacations. Our family loved soccer and we were always a part of the town league or school team growing up. We were all actually pretty good and my dad even coached our teams sometimes when he wasn't busy traveling. We used to really enjoy going on family vacations to Disney World in Florida, California, and Mexico. We even went on a Caribbean cruise once, which was a great experience.

A lot of these things that I went through as a child really taught me how to be a good father to my children. God allowed me to grow up not really having a good relationship with my dad because he wanted to be that Father to me. Now he has filled that void in my life. Knowing my heavenly Father and how much he loves me has now made up for all those years of not getting that from my dad. I'm not saying that my dad didn't love me, but he never really showed it. Maybe it's because he didn't know how to express his feelings. Nevertheless, God is amazing, and he is so much greater than any earthly father could ever be.

CHAPTER 2
HIGH SCHOOL AND HIP HOP

By the time I got to high school I was smoking cigarettes and weed. After school, Jason and I would hang out in the streets with friends, sometimes until late at night. By this time more black families had moved into West Hempstead and we had made a few friends. Almost all the friends we had in those days were black boys who were in similar situations as us. Their parents were professionals who worked a lot, so they had a lot of freedom and idle time to roam the streets getting in trouble.

We used to walk around West Hempstead drinking 40s which were big bottles of forty ounces of beer (for those who don't know). Back then this was the cool thing to do, drink 40s and get high. This is what we heard the rappers talk about in their music so that is what we did. We even started a little gang with a couple of the guys we hung out with who were from Hempstead. Hempstead was a neighboring city, but it was a lot different from West Hempstead. It was a lower-income city so there was a lot of poverty, gangs, and crime there.

This is when we really started to get in trouble because we were in the streets all the time doing stupid things. The cops in our town came to know who we were, especially because of Jason. He was always getting in trouble with the law for fighting, stealing, or something crazy. We grew up in a nice home, went to catholic/private schools, and my parents had money. The thing was that we never really got the things that other children had. Most people thought that we were spoiled but we didn't see it that way. We never had the cool new clothes, sneakers, or gadgets that other children had. My parents spent a lot of money on our education, but they didn't really buy us the things that we wanted. Therefore, we started to do bad things to get them.

We started stealing and shoplifting a lot, and Jason even started selling drugs. It wasn't until after getting caught a couple of times and almost going to jail that I realized stealing wasn't for me. At one point Jason had gotten arrested and went to jail for like 9 months. When I went to visit him, it was a wakeup call for me because I saw how easily our freedom could be lost. The crazy thing is that Jason actually seemed to enjoy getting locked up. I guess it gave him credibility in the streets, which was a big thing for him because he got worse after this.

The hip hop and rap songs we used to listen to and the videos we used to watch on tv actually glorified the life we were living. One of his favorite rappers was Tupac Shakur. My favorite rapper back then was Big E. Smalls. Drinking, smoking, getting locked up, getting women, and doing whatever it took to get money were the common themes in the music back then. It's funny that 20 plus years later the songs still talk about the same nonsense, but now it's much more intense.

When I got to 10th grade was when I met the love of my life and now beautiful wife, Grace. It was one summer night at a house party that Jason was having in our basement. Back then I was really into music. I even bought some nice turntables and a mixer and became a DJ. Sometimes I would do parties, but I really just liked playing records on the equipment alone in the basement of our house. I would stay down there for hours playing music with the volume up high. I had some heavy bass speakers so the whole house used to shake when the bass hit.

Proverbs 31:10 "10 Who can find a virtuous woman? for her price is far above rubies."

From the first time I met Grace I just knew that she would be my wife one day. You could say it was love at first sight. All I knew about her that day was that she was beautiful and that she went to a Catholic school in Hempstead with my brother. As I got to know her, I realized why I was going to marry her, she was the perfect woman for me. She was giving, kind, loving, affectionate, and just fun to be around. When she smiled it just brightened up the whole room. She was really the Grace of God that was sent to me.

I didn't know God at the time, but I know it was him who put it in me. However, in those days I wanted to be a playboy. The hip hop and rap songs never really glorified getting married, it was actually the opposite. So like the rappers, I wanted to get money, get high, and have lots of women around me. I didn't know God at the time, but I know it was him who put it in me to know that I would marry her one day.

Little did I know my Dad had other plans and was about to send me away to the island of Jamaica to go to school. Right around the same time, I had gotten hurt playing soccer and had to have surgery to have my hip pinned. This was my first time ever having surgery and it was a scary experience. My dad took me to, I believe, one of the best orthopedic surgeons in NY. So, the surgery went quickly and smoothly without any complications. Nevertheless, after the surgery I was in a very vulnerable state and I think this was the only reason I agreed to go to Jamaica.

My parents had finally figured out what the hip hop culture was doing to us. They were right because we definitely were being negatively influenced by it. Although sending us away was not the solution. They thought it was the right thing to do so in August of 1993, my dad flew me to Jamaica and left me there with my aunt in Kingston. My brother Jason was sent to military school in upstate New York because my parents didn't know what to do with him anymore. He had been expelled from multiple schools and was totally rebellious.

My time in Jamaica was one of my worst experiences growing up. Having my parents send me off to another country to live with family members that I barely knew was very tough. I went to a private school there with some rich kids. Coming from America to Jamaica made me, to them, a "Yankee" which they didn't like so again I was bullied. I was threatened a lot and I even almost got jumped, but God sent me a helper. I only had one friend in school there and his name was Gary. He stood up for me and got me out of that situation. Thank God!

I used to call home to my mother crying for her to let me come home, but she couldn't because she feared my dad. I clearly remember that Christmas, begging her to let me come home to be with my family for the holiday. I heard my dad come over to her, take the phone, and he hung up on me. I was only 15 years old and this was a traumatic time in my life.

Eventually after five or six months of me crying to my mother, she felt sorry for me. She was able to sneak me back home into the U.S. without my dad's approval. My dad was furious with her decision, but could not do anything because I was already home. Once I got home, I was adamant that I was not going back there. I agreed to go to military school instead which was another one of my dad's bad ideas. The school was called Randolph Macon Academy and it was in Virginia. It was still far away from home, but at least it was in the states and I got to come home on holidays.

Military school was supposed to teach me discipline, I guess. It was just like I saw in the movies. I had to wake up early every morning, my bed had to be made perfectly, my uniform had to be clean and pressed, and I had to be standing at attention outside my room by six in the morning or I got written up. After a certain amount of times getting written up, I had to do something called tours. Tours were when I had to march laps around the campus. I was always getting in trouble and doing tours which became a regular thing for me. It wasn't really because I was bad, I just wasn't used to all the strict rules and regulations.

I don't know why, but as a sophomore in high school I ended up having a senior for a roommate. Not only was he a senior but he was one of the biggest guys on the football team. So, I'm sure you can guess what happened... I was bullied again and even got beat up several times by him. He actually would verbally and physically attack me sometimes while I was sleeping. One day I got tired of getting bullied and to his surprise I actually beat him up. Shortly after this last time, he was transferred out of my room. Glory to God!

Romans 8:28 "And we know that all things work together for good to them that love God, to them who are the called according to his purpose."

When I look back, I know that God had his hand on my life all along. He had allowed me to keep getting into these situations to toughen me up. Through my whole life you will see that he was preparing me for the life that he would later call me into in his Kingdom. It was a call to live a life like Jesus lived. It is a victorious life, but also a life of rejection, abuse, and persecution. He wanted me to have no fear when I was going into the streets standing up for truth and against sin.

After my sophomore year was over, I was able to convince my parents to let me stay home. They were having so many problems with Jason that they really didn't care. I ended up back at a school called Portledge for eleventh grade. This was an expensive private school in Long Island that I had gone to in like eighth grade.

Now that summer in 1994 was when Grace and I officially became a couple, and my parents liked her a lot. We had spoken a couple of times during that very long year that I was away at these two other schools, but we didn't actually become boyfriend and girlfriend until I came back. I think us getting together may have also been part of the reason that my parents allowed me to stay in New York.

Grace lived like five minutes away from my house. Her parents both moved here from Puerto Rico and had a house in Hempstead. Grace went to Catholic school all her life and even worked in the same Catholic Church that my family would attend sometimes. She lived a very sheltered childhood and was not exposed to all the bad things that I was exposed to. So we were total opposites in many ways. I've heard it said that opposites attract which I think was true for us, just like with my mom and dad.

Many times, when I wanted to see her, I couldn't because her parents were so strict. Not only that, but they were racist also and didn't want her to be with me. They lived around and worked with mostly black people, but they did not want their little girl with a black boy. So I was not able to see her nearly as much as I wanted to which used to make me sad and upset. Sometimes I would have to ride my bike to her house in the middle of the night just to see her. She would sneak me into her room by me climbing through her window. It was a good thing that her bedroom was on the first floor. I didn't have to do a lot of acrobatics to get into her window.

CHAPTER 3
MY INTRODUCTION TO THE PARTY LIFE

I ended up graduating from West Hempstead High School in 1996 after having gone to five different high schools. After my 18th birthday, my dad decided to kick me out of the house. I had told him that I wanted to take a year off from school. I did not want to go to college right away, but he was not having it. Things were never the same between us since he sent me to Jamaica. I was very bitter about the whole thing and I resented him for it. I think he probably knew it, so he just wanted me out of his house.

When he told me to move out, I had nowhere to go. I was scared and didn't know how I would make it on my own. Thank God my mother had compassion on me again and did not let me go into the streets. She helped me to get my first apartment which was in the next town over called Franklin Square. It was a nice one-bedroom basement apartment. The best thing about it was that I now had my own place. I was a young guy with a beautiful girlfriend, nice car, a job, and my own place. In my eyes I had everything that a guy my age could want so I was the man.

Now that I was not with my parents anymore, not going to school, and had a girlfriend I couldn't see that often, I had a lot of free time. So naturally after a while, with me being a worldly guy, I started to look for other ways to enjoy myself. I started going to roller skating parties and then going to teen nightclubs. From there I became addicted to partying. The more I watched videos on MTV and BET the more I wanted the life I saw these rappers and entertainers living. At first, I was only going out once a month, then it went to once a week, until it became a few nights a week. I would always find a party or a club to go to and this became my passion and addiction for the next almost twenty years of my life.

Clubbing gave me the excitement that I wanted in my life. I also got the attention that I wanted, but couldn't get from my parents or my girlfriend. I was a decent looking guy and I knew how to dress. Therefore, I got attention when I went out. When I first started partying, I would go out with Jason or one of my friends from the neighborhood. My brother and my friends were all fairly good-looking young guys and at one point our little crew started calling ourselves Long Island's Most Wanted.

I used to have so many crazy nights out partying that it's a miracle that I am even still alive. I drove countless nights back and forth from Long Island to the city, drunk and high. It was like thirty to forty minutes away from where we lived, but we used to speed and make it there in like twenty minutes. Manhattan was my favorite place to party because there were so many places to go to. I used to frequent places like Copa Cabana, Latin Quarters, and Vertigo because at the time, my friends and I were into Latin women. Growing up around mostly white and Spanish people, it was only natural.

I remember one night my friends and I were leaving a nightclub in the city. It might have been Palladium which was one of my favorite clubs to go to. I remember seeing the R&B group Total perform there. Anyways, some other guys that I knew were in two other cars and they left the city a few minutes before us. There used to be car shows in front of the clubs so that could have been why we didn't leave the city with our other friends that night.

I used to love flossing (showing off) with my car in front of the club after it was over. Also, it was a good time to get girls phone numbers, which was a big thing for us back then. My buddies and I used to compete to see which of us could get the most numbers. Little did I know it wasn't me wanting to floss or get numbers that night that kept me from leaving with my friends. It was God protecting me from what was to come.

If I remember correctly, we were on the Long Island Expressway headed back home early in the morning. We were all drunk, and while driving, we came upon an accident ahead of us that looked like it had just happened. When we slowed down and got closer to the scene, we saw both of our friends had crashed their cars into each other and another car.

At the time I was driving a 1992 money green Infiniti Q45. I had worked several different jobs and saved up my money to buy it. I loved that car and at that time it was one of the fastest luxury sedans on the road. One of the cars involved in the accident which was my friend Roger's car was also a Q45. Since we had these kinds of fast cars, my friends and I would always race each other on the highways and this night was no different.

That night Roger let someone else drive his car for him and he sat in the passenger seat because he was too drunk. Unfortunately, he ended up dying in the accident, while the driver lived. One of the passengers in the other car was ejected from the car and ended up twenty feet away from the scene. Having never seen a dead body, it was one of the scariest things I had ever seen. I saw my friend Roger's eyes rolled back in his head. He was hanging out of his car, dead. It was a sobering experience for me. One minute we were all in clubs in the city partying, then the next minute two of them were dead and gone.

Romans 6:23 "For the wages of sin is death; but the gift of God is eternal life through Jesus Christ our Lord."

As I write these things the Holy Spirit is reminding me of a reggae song that I used to listen to all the time called "Living Dangerously". It's ironic because if I only knew how dangerous I was actually living. Not only was I constantly taking risks with my life and others, but with my soul as well. If I had left that club ten minutes earlier, I could have lost my life and went to hell. God's grace and mercy kept me!

Not only did I survive countless nights of drinking and driving, but also many fights and brawls. Some of which people ended up getting stabbed and even shot right in front of me. One of the guys that I used to party with after high school was a hot tempered mulatto (half black and half white) guy named Dean. We had a lot in common and ended up becoming best friends for a while. We both wore big chains and we got a lot of attention when we went out. We loved to drive around in our cars flossing and blasting r&b, hip hop, and reggae music. I used to change up cars almost yearly, but when I had my Q45 he was driving a Lexus.

Growing up in New York back in the 1990s, you always had to be ready for a fight. Especially with rap music exploding on the scene. Every young guy wanted to be like either BIG E, DMX, or Tupac.

I remember one night a group of us went to a nightclub in the city. At one point in the night Dean had gone to the bathroom by himself. It was not a smart idea because we had never been to this place before and we could tell we were not wanted as soon as we got there. A few minutes later he comes stumbling out of the bathroom dripping blood from his face. Some guys in the bathroom had sliced his face with a knife and snatched his chain off his neck. This was a very common occurrence back then. Usually, the guys who had the big chains and nice cars, were targets for thieves or what were called back then stickup kids. I used to walk around with a big chain and lots of jewelry for many years, but by the grace of God I was never robbed.

After Dean told us what had happened, we went looking for the guys. It was about five or six of us that night and we ended up getting into a brawl outside of the club with these guys. I ended up fighting a guy who had some kind of blade in his hand, and he started swinging at me. Eventually these guys ended up running away but not until after we landed a few blows on them. The situation could have been much worse if one of those guys had a gun. Jason also wanted to get his gun from my car, but thank God I didn't let him. Someone could have died, or we could have all gone to jail that night. I remember having a couple of splashes of blood on my Timberland boots when I got home but that was it. This was just one of many bloody events that took place during my years of partying and being in the streets. I have seen many people get knocked out, arrested, and hospitalized at nightclubs.

We used to go to the Tunnel nightclub in NYC which was one of the most gangster clubs in the city back then. People would frequently get robbed, stabbed, and shot there, but we continued to go because it was the place to be on a Sunday night. A lot of the rappers I looked up to used to perform and hang out there. One night I remember seeing Jay Z and Memphis Bleek perform which was big for me because they were some of my favorite artists or even idols back then.

I was addicted to that life of drinking and partying. My drink of choice in my younger years was Old English 40s or other beers. As I matured in my clubbing game I graduated to hard liquor and then to champagne. This was when buying bottles of champagne became the cool thing to do and it was in all the rap songs.

One year, my older half-brother Peter on my Dad's side invited me to go with him to Cancun, Mexico to Puff Daddy's All-Star Weekend. He actually worked for a party promotion company that did big events. It was a big deal for me as I got to party with a lot of the stars that I saw on TV. I also got to spend some time with my older brother which I didn't do often. I remember being at one of the nightclubs in Cancun and I saw a young black guy buying what looked like cases and cases of champagne. I was mesmerized and had to go ask my brother who that was, spending all that money. He looked at me like I was crazy and asked, "you don't know who that is? That's Allen Iverson and he just got signed to the NBA." I wasn't a big sport's fan at the time and didn't really know who the star players were. I did see people like P. Diddy and Mase, who I knew were some of the hottest artists at the time and the number of women they were getting. During that trip, I got a glimpse of the life that these sports stars and entertainers were living, and I wanted it.

That weekend really took my partying to another level. Shortly after that I started traveling to other states to party. I had a fake I.D and would go to twenty-one and even twenty-three and over clubs when I was only like 19. My buddies and I also started going to Miami Beach for Spring Break every year. I had a group of Spanish and white friends that I would go down there with. Then I had my other group of black friends, who I grew up with, that I went to other events with. Such as, Philly Greek Fest, Morehouse Homecoming in Atlanta, NBA All Star Wknd wherever it was that year, and Grant's Tomb in NYC.

For several years I worked full time in different restaurants mainly as a waiter and I made good money. The good thing for me about it was that I brought home tips every day, so every day was like payday. I would use that money to go partying at night. I was also into buying and fixing up cars and selling them for profit. I became obsessed with cars and was always known around town for the nice hooked up cars I used to drive. Almost every year I would upgrade to a new car. Then I would spend time and money putting rims, stereo equipment, flashing lights, and other things in the car. People used to think it was my parents who bought me these cars, but it wasn't.

My mother had always been there for me when I needed her, but she only bought me my first car. She bought me a 1994 Nissan Sentra the year that my dad kicked me out. We got a great deal on it at an auto auction out in Long Island. I quickly hooked it up with my own money and flipped it for almost double what she had paid for it. I then bought a sweet Nissan Maxima with white pinstriped seats which I loved. I always put nice rims on my cars because having a nice car with rims was a big deal in New York back then. After switching up cars a couple of times I ended up with the Infiniti Q45. I put 19-inch rims on it and that was the last car that I paid for all cash.

I'd been following and trying to keep up with the hip hop culture and its trends. After this, big trucks became popular and I decided to get a truck. I used to always listen to Hot 97 and one of my favorite DJs on there was Funk Master Flex. He used to talk about big trucks all the time and it made me want to get one. So, in 2001, Grace and I leased our first car together and it was a white Lincoln Navigator which I quickly put 20-inch rims on. This was my first time having a car payment. With Grace's help I was able to pay the six hundred dollar a month payment for the next three years. Back then that was a lot of money to pay for a car. She was working full time at a bank and going to college at the time. I was very blessed to be able to do a lot of the things that the "ballers," were doing without selling drugs or being famous. A lot of the help that I got was from "girlfriends" who always had good jobs. My mom was also always there to help me when I needed her.

I was also always a very fashionable guy and I liked to wear the hottest new clothes. I used to buy a lot of Polo and was constantly in the store buying new outfits to wear to the clubs. I remember when the throwback jerseys became popular. I would go out and spend hundreds of dollars at a time just to buy one jersey.

After a while I became known among my peers for bottle popping. At first, I would always make sure that my party funds included being able to buy bottles of Hennessy and Moët. Then when I started to make more money, I stepped it up and would buy more expensive bottles of champagne like Crystal. On an average night of partying I would spend between one and five hundred dollars and this went on for many years. At one point some of the friends that I had been partying with stopped wanting to go out with me. They were regular guys with regular jobs like me and after one or two nights going out, they would be broke for weeks. This did not stop me though, I was so hooked to the lifestyle. When I spent all my money, I would find a way to get more money to keep going out. It was an addiction.

It is so sad the amount of money I spent trying to keep up with the ballers and the rappers. Especially when it comes to partying and alcohol. When I look back over all those almost 20 years of partying, I know I've spent multiple tens of thousands of dollars. That is a lot of money for a regular guy. What a waste!!

I was brainwashed into this mindset that I had. All I cared about was looking good, making money, partying, cars, and women. Again, it is only by the grace of God that Grace didn't leave me considering I was living this playboy lifestyle. She didn't really know about all the things I was doing, but people would tell her bad things about me. She loved me so much that she would not believe the things she would hear, even though many times they were true. I did love her, but I was a bad boy and I knew that I didn't deserve her.

CHAPTER 4
FAMILY TIME

As the years went by my brother Jason took a different route and went into the gang life. He joined a gang known as the Bloods, one of America's biggest gangs. By this time my youngest brother, Gordon had been sent to Jamaica to live. My parents said that we were a bad influence on him, and they were probably right. Jason continued to get in trouble with the law and I was a womanizing party animal. Our family had grown apart and we barely spoke to each other.

Eventually Jason had a daughter named Nina with his longtime girlfriend Jessica. Nina was such a blessing to our family and when I was with her, I treated her like she was my own. Jason loved his daughter and tried to make it work with her mom, but things were always off. My brother had a lot of issues that none of us knew how to deal with. I know now that he had a lot of demons because of the life he was living. He had moved down south and became a stick-up kid, robbing people for drugs and money. I was scared to be around him sometimes when I went to visit him because at any minute we could be in a shootout.

Sadly in 2002 my brother Jason took his own life leaving his girlfriend and three-year-old daughter behind. My mom was on the phone with him when it happened, and it was really tough for her to deal with. The way it happened at first we thought that someone had killed him. Later we concluded that he did commit suicide. The police had originally ruled it a suicide, but we didn't believe it until we had our own investigation done.

Unfortunately, my brother was not saved and didn't know the Lord. He did have a small Bible that he carried around and probably read it occasionally, but he certainly didn't live by it. I know now that I will never see him again. Even though at the time I thought I would see him in heaven because I didn't know any better. It was a sad time for our family. Unfortunately, Jason's death did not bring us closer together like deaths sometimes do for families.

Then in 2002 a few months before Jason's death I had my first son named Amani and it was one of the greatest moments of my life. I really enjoyed being a father and I would take my son everywhere with me. I was now able to give Amani the attention that I wished that my dad had given me. I soon started to come under the conviction that I had to change my ways. Not only because I wanted to be a great father, but because I had a family member that I loved, die prematurely. I now started to realize how fragile life was and I wanted to be around to watch my son grow up.

Anyone can have a baby and be a dad but it's a lot harder to be a father. I actually had learned how to be a father by watching all the things that my dad used to do and not do with me and my brothers. My dad was not really around much when I was younger. Even when he was around there was no real personal connection between us. He never really tried to get to know me and he didn't show me any kind of affection. In fact, growing up I don't remember either of my parents ever telling me that they loved me. Don't get me wrong I know that they did love me, but they obviously did not know how to show it.

Growing up I used to always go to my friend Andrew's house who was a Columbian kid who lived across the street from us. He was my best friend in my elementary school days and later he became the best man at my wedding. I used to always be jealous of him because his parents would always show him affection. They would tell him they loved him all the time. His parents were professionals like mine and worked a lot, but you could feel the love between them, and I wanted that.

In high school I used to spend a lot of time at my friends Robert and Ron's house who lived across town. Jason and I had met them at a Catholic school that we used to attend called St. Paul. They had a big family and always had their cousins, aunts, and uncles over their house. They had a strong family bond and you could feel the love that they had for each other. I remember during Christmas time they used to put on a family play and it was really something special to see.

At the time I did not know what it was that was drawing me to want to be in other people's homes. Looking back, I know that it was the feeling of love and family that was so comforting. My brothers and I did not really have that growing up. My cousin Christopher came up from Jamaica to live with us for a while at one point but that was pretty much all the family that we had come over. I did have family members that lived in Long Island, but my parents were always too busy to hang out with them.

When I got older and was able to drive, I started hanging out at my cousin's house in Westbury. They had a big family with six children and I always wanted to get to know them more, so I did. Jackson, David, and Ann were the oldest and closest to my age, so I hung out with them mostly. I loved being at their house especially when my aunt Rochelle was cooking. She owned a restaurant and made some great Jamaican food. Again, there was that sense of love and family there that I didn't feel at home.

My brothers and I always had everything we needed. We had food, clothes, shelter, and education from some of the best Catholic, private, and military schools. The fact that I did not get the affection and family bonding that these other families had was not by accident. God was creating in me a hunger for a family of my own that I could experience this with and now I had started my own family.

Soon after Amani was born, I started working as a loan officer at a mortgage company and I was making good money. This was right before the housing and mortgage boom. At this time, I was renting a room in a house in Queens, Ny. Grace and I after like 8 years, finally decided to find an apartment and move in together. She was working full time at an Insurance company and going to college in the evenings, so I spent a lot of time taking care of Amani. I would even take him to work with me sometimes. I was still enjoying the nightlife but not as much due to my new responsibilities.

The apartment we got was out in Amityville, Long Island. One of Grace's friends helped us to get the apartment. It was not in the greatest of areas which we quickly came to find out. Shortly after we moved in, we got robbed. One morning I came outside of our apartment and found our Lincoln Navigator sitting on bricks. I had recently upgraded the rims from 20s to 22-inch rims which were very expensive, and they got stolen. I was one of the few people in that area at the time with a truck sitting on 22s, so it was a big deal for me, and I was in shock. Not only that this happened to me but that it happened literally the same night as my brother's death. It couldn't have happened at a worse time. If there was a silver lining in this, it was that I had kept the old rims that I originally had on the truck. So, I just put those back on, but it was a very trying time to say the least.

After this incident we quickly started looking to move out of there. Grace and I were making good money and a few months later we were blessed to be able to buy our first home together. It's funny that God used Grace's dad to help us buy the house. After he saw that I was getting serious with his daughter and we started having children he accepted me.

We bought a five-bedroom high-ranch house in Deer Park, Ny which was further out on Long Island from where we grew up. During this time banks were giving out mortgages like hot cakes, so we were able to purchase a home with very little money down.

We loved our new home and it had a legal rental apartment downstairs, so we started renting it out. We became landlords and soon after I got the idea to start investing in real estate. I ended up buying another high ranch home a few blocks away that was similar to ours. We did some work on the house and made it into two apartments and rented them out. We now had three sets of tenants and we were making extra money off the rents.

My parents had decided to buy a home in South Florida around this time. I was still holding that resentment for my dad in my heart, but I still stayed connected because of my mom. It was all part of God's plan because I had been going to Miami for years partying during Spring break. I loved Florida and when my parents bought a home there, I quickly brought Grace down there to show her the place. It was a beautiful home in a private gated community in Davie, Fl. One Christmas when we went down there to visit my parent's house. I took her to Ft. Lauderdale beach and proposed to her on the beach. We both fell in love with the place and we soon after made up our minds to move to Florida.

Grace and I were tired of the New York hustle and bustle lifestyle. We had been together for 10 years at this point and she was pregnant with our daughter Sanai. It was time to take our relationship to the next level. Living the playboy life and trying to have a family at the same time was getting tough for me. I had had other girlfriends, some of them for years at a time but it was time for me to grow up. I didn't really want to get married yet however I knew that Grace was the one and I did not want her to get away. I figured it was time when she started asking me why I had not asked her to marry me. She was a beautiful, loving woman and I began to wonder what I was waiting for.

Somehow, I knew that the life we were living was not going to last if we didn't get married. I had been cheating on her all along and she had also cheated on me a couple of times as well. When I found out I got upset but how could I blame her. I used to always hear what goes around, comes around. Grace, who was a sweet and innocent girl. Had slowly over time been somewhat corrupted by the world also. I'm sure my infidelity contributed to it as well, but the culture played a big part. You see she was not into hard rap music like I was, but she came to love R&B which was just as bad. The typical R&B songs actually promoted and glorified cheating on your mate, especially when they mess up.

It is crazy how much even the television shows glorified this behavior. I remember one crazy show that I believe brainwashed a lot of people. It was called Sex in the City. This TV "program" was totally demonic and sadly it was a big hit for many years. I used to hear people say all the time; you are what you eat. I do believe that, but I also believe that you become what you listen to and you become what you watch. Why do you think the enemy (the devil) is trying to get everyone hooked on watching porn? It is because he knows that the more people who watch it, the more sexual perversion and sin there will be. I was hooked on porn for many years and I believe it contributed greatly to my ungodly lifestyle.

2 Corinthians 2:11 "Lest Satan should get an advantage of us: for we are not ignorant of his devices."

The fact that Grace and I were not saved and did not know Jesus yet gave us no chance against the devil's brainwashing devices. The Bible says that the devil is the prince of the power of the air. The enemy knows how influential TV and radio are so he controls most of what people see and hear. He pushes his agenda to manipulate and brainwash the masses into living for him in sin and not living righteously for God.

Ephesians 2:2 "Wherein in time past ye walked according to the course of this world, according to the prince of the power of the air, the spirit that now worketh in the children of disobedience"

CHAPTER 5
THE DEVIL'S PLAN DIDN'T WORK

Mark 10:9 "What therefore God hath joined together, let not man put asunder."

During the first ten years before we got married, we had so many people try to come between us it is not even funny. When I look back at all the incidents and crazy stuff we have been through, I see that it was God's supernatural power at work that was keeping us together for all those years.

The devil tried to do everything possible to split us up. I remember back in our high school days that Grace's friends were always trying to get her to break up with me. Whenever we had a fight, she would be upset for days sometimes. So, her girlfriends would constantly be in her ear asking her why she puts up with me and telling her to leave me. Mind you none of her friends really had boyfriends. It is funny that it's always the people that don't have relationship experience who try to give relationship advice… It got so bad at times that even friends that she had known since elementary school actually gave her an ultimatum to choose me or them.

As a matter of fact, just a few years ago we found a letter that Grace got a long time ago. It was from her best friend way back then. In the letter she called me all kinds of names and even said that I would give Grace a sexually transmitted disease if she stayed with me. Praise God that that curse that was spoken against us never came to pass. Our relationship was under constant attack by her friends, neighbors, and even her parents. The devil tried everything in the book to break us up, but nothing worked.

Grace's parents were racist and were not happy with our relationship. They did not want their daughter with a black guy, and they would make comments about me all the time. I remember one-time Grace telling me that her mother asked her: are you going to have that monkey's babies? Referring to me as a monkey! I was hurt when she told me this and it was etched into my mind forever. I have long since forgiven them, but something like that you never forget.

I had been used to dealing with racism all my life especially growing up in a predominantly white neighborhood. Especially with me going to mostly white schools but this situation was tough for me. Knowing that this is the woman I wanted to be with for the rest of my life, but her family was racist. Even her sister Carla went to great lengths to try to break us up also. She used the fact that her parents didn't like me against Grace. Carla was older than Grace and I believe was just jealous of her because again she had no real relationship of her own. She really hated me with a passion, and she showed it.

One time she hired a private investigator to follow me and investigate my life. This private investigator followed me around for weeks documenting all the dirt I was doing.

At the time I was also in a relationship with a girl named Ashley who I had met at a nightclub a few years prior. I spent a lot more time with her because she was free. Grace was always on lockdown at home with her strict parents. Ashley treated me well, bought me things, and helped me pay my bills, but she wasn't the one that God had chosen for me to marry.

The private investigator took pictures and got video recordings of me out with her. They even got us kissing and everything. I was caught red handed but I still denied to Grace that the girl in the video meant anything to me. I think I learned that from old players like my dad that if you get caught; deny, deny, deny. When I was younger, I used to hear my mom asking my dad about dealing with other women and he would always simply deny any wrongdoing. Lie, lie, lie….

People used to tell me all the time that I looked just like my dad. I never saw it but in this way, I was just like him. I was a dog and liked having multiple girlfriends. I was not the kind of guy that would go out looking for one-night stands. I never had a prostitute or paid for sex even though I was exposed to many people who were in that lifestyle. Having steady girlfriends was my thing. Having two or three at a time was a normal thing for me for many years. These girls didn't know about each other. I don't know how I pulled it off for so long, but now I got caught. When I look back on my life, I am so ashamed of how I treated these women and especially my wife. I thank God for his grace, mercy, and forgiveness. I was a fool.

In regard to the private investigator's findings. It turned out that Grace loved me so much that she stayed with me even after having proof that I was cheating on her. That was God again because other times people would tell her that they saw me out with women, but now she saw it with her own eyes. After this incident, her family pretty much gave up trying to split us up. They figured that at this point if that video couldn't do it, nothing could. God had a plan for both of us and nothing could stop it!

CHAPTER 6
TIME TO MAN UP

Proverbs 18:22 "Whoso findeth a wife findeth a good thing, and obtaineth favour of the LORD."

In 2004 after Grace finished college and got her bachelor's degree, we got married. My dad owned a restaurant at the time, so we had our wedding reception there. My mother was paying for the wedding and us having it there, saved her a lot of money. A few months later our daughter Sanai was born, and it was now time for me to hang up my player shoes. I now had my beautiful little girl and my handsome boy, a matching pair so I was set. Soon after this I cut off all the previous relationships that I had been in and I actually started being faithful to my wife. I had become a husband, a father of 2, and a real estate investor. I wanted to take my life more seriously. Being rich and successful was my goal and I wanted only the best for me and my family. We wore nice clothes, we had a nice house, jewelry, and luxury cars.

When the lease was up on the Navigator I was driving, we gave it back. I then was able to get a great deal at the auction on a 2002 white BMW 745i with only ten thousand miles on it. I even got a deal on some nice 22-inch rims for it. We had also bought Grace an emerald green Jaguar S type. We were living a lavish lifestyle again trying to keep up with the Joneses and the hip hop culture. The BMW 745 was pretty much the hottest car out and I felt like a king driving it on the streets of NY. There were quite a few songs out at the time that mentioned this car, but my favorite was "Lean Back" by a rapper named Fat Joe. A 745 was the featured car in his video, so I felt really special because I had one.

Around this time, my parents bought a second home in South Florida for when they retired. Eventually Grace and I decided to move down there. We refinanced our two houses in New York and took the equity out and bought a house in Miramar, Florida.

We both had lived in New York all our lives and we were ready for a change. Also, it was getting more and more depressing to us in NY with all the crime and the bad weather. Sometimes during the winter, you could go for weeks without seeing any sunshine. Mind you by this time I had been going to Miami, the sunshine state, for years to party. So, I would get a taste of the abundant sunshine, beautiful weather, palm trees, and relaxing lifestyle. Then I would have to come back to the hustle and bustle grinding life in NY. For me there was no comparison between the two. Also, I was now raising children and wanted a better life for them. Don't get me wrong, I loved New York, but the quality of life was much better in South Florida.

In 2005 we bought a five-bedroom and three-bathroom home that was almost three thousand square feet. The house had a beautiful pool and it was on a lake. It was about ten minutes away from my parent's house in Davie. Originally, I had bought the home to try to flip it and make money but that never happened. We ended up falling in love with it and spent the next eleven years of our life there.

The house was in West Miramar, which was twenty minutes from Miami Beach, arguably the biggest party destination in the world. I was still into partying but had slowed down my partying substantially. I went out occasionally and when I did it was usually when one of my friends named Harry came down to visit me. He had moved from NY to Tampa like a year before I moved down. My parents also had brought my youngest brother Gordon back to America and he was living in their house in Davie, Florida. So, I also went out with him sometimes.

I was living in paradise with my beautiful family, a beautiful home, 2 rental properties in NY, two luxury cars, and money in the bank. Life could not get much better for me and I felt like a million bucks. In a few short years we had made close to a half a million dollars. Most of which went into keeping up this baller lifestyle that I was seeing in the rap videos and wanted to maintain living.

In 2008 however things started to get rocky for us when one by one our tenants in NY stopped paying us rent. Being an absentee landlord started to take a toll on me. I was constantly flying back and forth to NY to go to court to evict tenants. This was in the middle of the financial crisis of 2007-2008, when people started losing their jobs. A couple of years later, both houses in NY eventually went into foreclosure due to our inability to pay the mortgages. That income that I was getting from the rentals stopped. My plan to be a real estate investor had to be put on hold.

We had taken an adjustable rate mortgage on our house in Miramar when we bought it which was a big mistake. The banks were letting people buy homes with exceptionally low interest rates just to get them in the home. However, after a few years the rate would shoot up to a much higher rate. So, when our interest rate reset at a much higher rate, our mortgage payment went up by over a thousand dollars. Then in 2009 Grace lost her job at the Insurance company that she was working at so things really got bad.

We had an outrageous mortgage payment of around four thousand dollars a month with taxes and insurance. We were also paying around two thousand a month in car payments and car insurance. Just before she lost her job, we had traded in the 745 at the BMW dealership. They then financed us the BMW 750Li which was almost the same car but newer and a little bit longer. Again, following the trend of the day and trying to keep up with my lavish lifestyle I continued to stretch myself. This was a stressful time and things were not as perfect as they had been. I had always smoked weed, but I began smoking, drinking, and partying more often to numb myself from the reality of what was going on. It had been like once or twice a month I would go out for a few years, but now I was going out pretty much every weekend.

Grace eventually found another job and I found a job working for a loan modification company. It's funny that before the financial crisis I would help people to get loans from banks to buy homes. Then after the crisis I helped people to stop those same banks from taking their homes from them. I was making decent money, but I wanted to make more so I started working long hours.

I was only really trying to make more money so I could buy more bottles when I went to the club on the weekends. After years of drinking my tolerance had gone way up and champagne wouldn't get me drunk anymore. So, my drink of choice became Grey Goose vodka. I would buy a bottle or two almost every time I went to a club, again to keep up the baller image I had created for myself. You see, the cool guys in the clubs who got all the girls were the ones who were buying bottles especially in Miami. If you weren't popping bottles, it's like you were considered a nobody because that's all the rap songs talked about. The more bottles you popped, the more money people thought you had and the more women and attention you got. Every time there was a special occasion like my birthday, I would buy maybe four or five bottles, depending on how many people I was with. I went out so often that I would get discounts and sometimes even free bottles.

One year my dad who was retired and living in the house in Davie bought into an energy drink business. My mom still had her law practice in NY and wasn't ready to retire yet, so she came down like once a month. I was a mama's boy and I would talk to her on the phone every couple of days. My dad and I were ok with each other but didn't really see each other often. Even though he only lived like ten minutes away. One day he called me and asked me if I wanted to help him promote this new energy drink that he bought into, and I was shocked. He had never really asked me to help him do anything before.

The job entailed me going to stores, markets, and clubs trying to get them to buy and sell this energy drink. I wanted to make extra money and I was already going to clubs, so I figured hey why not. I wasn't into energy drinks, but it did taste better than most of the other ones that were on the market. So, we were actually able to get it into quite a few places in South Florida.

It was a lot of work, but it was a good experience for me and of course God had a purpose in it. One day I met a Rastafarian named Dave who was also promoting this same energy drink here in South Florida with my dad. We had a lot in common. We both had long dreads, loved to smoke weed, and both wanted to make a lot of money. Dave was married with like ten children by three or four different women. We quickly became friends and started to hang out.

Little did I know that God was going to use him to start planting seeds in me. Sometimes he would talk about the Bible and God. Other times I would call him, and he would tell me that he was meditating or praying. Eventually we started to have deep conversations and he would tell me about the corruption and lies in this world. It was usually while we were smoking, and at first, I thought he was making up stuff because he was high. As time went on, the things that he was saying started to make sense. After I believe a couple of years of promoting that energy drink, my dad stopped it for financial reasons. Dave and I had put a lot of time and effort into promoting it, so we were kind of upset.

CHAPTER 7
MY DOWNWARD SPIRAL

By this time Grace and I had stopped paying our mortgage because we just couldn't afford it anymore. After we didn't pay it for many months, the bank started the foreclosure process on our home. At the time I was working for a Law Firm, whose specialty was doing mortgage modification. Thank God, I had learned how to delay, stop, and even cancel foreclosures. So, we were able to delay and even get our foreclosure process canceled a couple of times. The bank had to completely start over the foreclosure process on our home more than once, which was a blessing for us. Every time they had to start over, it bought us almost another year. Nevertheless, it was still a stressful thing to go through and it started weighing on me.

Then one night, I think I hurt my shoulder or something and went to the hospital. I don't even remember what I went in for, but when the nurses checked my heart rate. They said that I had an irregular heartbeat, and they quickly rushed me in to see the doctors. The doctors then told me that there could be something wrong with my heart. They said that I needed to have an invasive procedure to check it. They scared me into doing the procedure. They told me that if I didn't do it, I could go into sudden cardiac arrest and die. After hearing this, in my mind, I had no choice. They quickly scheduled me at another hospital for the procedure and rushed me over there in an ambulance.

At the time, I did not know any better and thought that I could trust the doctors because they knew everything. I later found out that this is not the case and that doctors are just "practicing" medicine. Many times, they are just guessing what is wrong with people because they don't exactly know. That's why they run a whole bunch of tests to try to come up with their best guess. Sometimes you will even see doctors putting symptoms in google to try to find out what's wrong with a person.

Anyways after this procedure called a cardiac catheterization, where they stuck some wire in me and played around with my heart. They told me that they found nothing wrong with my heart and that I was fine and sent me home. However, a couple of days after I left the hospital, I started having erratic blood pressure readings. One day my pressure would be high. The next day it would be normal and the next day it would get really low and I would feel tired and weak. This went on for months and it sent me into a spiraling depression. Piled on top of all the other things I was stressed out about, I started losing a lot of weight and I thought I was going to die.

When I think back on that couple of days that I was in the hospital which was one of the scariest times in my life. I believe a spirit of death came on me in that hospital. During that experience, I felt such anxiety and fear. I had my wife, children, and family there in the hospital with me, but I still felt such fear. Now that I am saved and know the truth. When I visit hospitals to pray for sick people, I can see that the spiritual atmosphere in many hospitals is very demonic.

John 10:10 "The thief cometh not, but for to steal, and to kill, and to destroy: I am come that they might have life, and that they might have it more abundantly."

I believe the hospitals are second on the list of places where Satan kills the most people, right behind abortion clinics. People go there in their time of need and often get treated terribly. Then many leave and get worse than when they originally came in. They usually leave with a bunch of prescriptions for medication that will eventually cause other complications in their body. I also believe that in more times than we know about, people go in for simple problems and end up dead. I have heard of quite a few situations like that.

I am not saying that all hospitals are bad or that everyone that works in a hospital is evil. Many people have gotten the help that they needed in hospitals, me included. God does use doctors, nurses, and hospitals to heal people. I just believe we, especially here in America, are so quick to run to doctors and hospitals when we get sick. We should really be going to God first. I turn to Jesus Christ and pray for my healing before I go to the medical system for help.

If people only knew the power of prayer and the power that we have over sickness and disease in Christ. A lot of things would be different here in America and people would have more faith in God. People in many other countries trust God more because they don't have the luxury of free health care, medication, and hospitals everywhere. A lot of times, especially in third world countries people either; pray and trust God for their healing, they go to the witch doctor for help, or they die.

2 Corinthians 10:4 "For the weapons of our warfare are not carnal, but mighty through God to the pulling down of strong holds."

Many of the sicknesses and diseases that people are dealing with are spiritual conditions and can be taken care of or healed through prayer. Jesus cast demons out of people, and they were healed. Many people and even believers are ignorant to this fact. The fact that demons can and do cause sickness and disease.

So, getting back to the story. Things really went downhill fast for me after my hospital incident. I became more and more like a zombie and I thought my life was over. I remember I used to call my mother all the time telling her that I was gonna die but she never took me seriously. Grace would hear me say it, but I don't think she really realized what was going on with me. There were times that I would just stay in bed for days just eating, sleeping, and watching music videos.

The worse I felt about myself the more I went out and partied and as the years went by, I became numb to everything. I would take my children to school during the week and pick them up after, but I really was not there with them. My mind was only on getting high, partying, and getting women. On the weekends I would get high and drunk and then sleep the days away.

Partying became my life again and eventually I was going out so much I started to neglect my family. The club life became so intoxicating to me, especially with the music which seemed to be gaining stronger influence over society through the years. The attention I was getting from being the man on the club scene and from women, was what made me feel better about myself. That is all I saw in the music videos. So that's all that mattered was having fun and enjoying my life. One of the main slogans at the time was YOLO (You only live once). I was thinking that my life was going to end any day so I wanted to enjoy every day, no matter the consequences.

I never even thought about what my reckless behavior was doing to my wife. I didn't know that Grace was confused and had been feeling neglected for years. Eventually she started talking to one of her married coworkers who had been preying on her for a while. I found out about it one night when I looked at her phone. I saw a strange number and when I called it, a guy picked up. Turns out this guy was a so-called "believer". He talked to her about the Bible, but then was messing around with a married woman at work. I have learned since then, that many people who call themselves believers today, are not really believers. True Christians obey the Bible, which is very clear about adultery, which is basically, cheating on your spouse. It says that those who do such things cannot enter the Kingdom of God. Unless they repent, which basically means to change your ways and stop doing such things.

So naturally when I found out about this I was crushed. Especially on top of everything else I was going through; all I could do was cry. With how I was treating her and the enemy attacking her mind, it was bound to happen at some point. The good thing I guess, was that it only lasted a short time and I was able to catch her, before they could sleep together. So, when I confronted her about it, she cut off talking to the guy right away and quit that job. She told me that she didn't want to leave me, she was just feeling neglected at home. Hence, the enemy came in to tempt her at work and she fell for it.

That day, Grace and I agreed that she would never work in Corporate America again. We both learned a valuable lesson from this. We saw through the enemy's plan to separate and destroy marriages. Over the years, Grace would always tell me about her coworkers, who were cheating on their spouses at work. This is unfortunately a very common thing in the workplace, and it is the cause of many divorces. One of Grace's ex bosses, who had been hitting on her years prior to this. He told her that he would leave his wife if she left me and went out with him. Sadly, this is the culture that we are living in today. People could care less anymore about the sanctity of marriage. Not only here in America, but all over the world and it's all the work of the devil. People don't want to obey God's word, so it's only natural that the enemy takes over the minds of the people.

There is a reason why the devil pushes the feminist agenda here in America. It is mainly to break up the family unit. If a woman is single or has no children it is different, but I believe that God has a divine order for his families and the way that his families should be run. The man is the one who should do what he can to provide for his wife and children. Not saying the wife is supposed to just sit around and do nothing. If she has free time, she could start a home-based business or something. However, her main priority should be to take care of her husband, the children, and the household. This is, I believe one of, if not the most important job anyone can have. Most women back in the days knew this and that was their focus and families stayed together. Nowadays women aren't domestic anymore and don't want to stay home. Sadly, many don't even want to have children, or know how to cook and clean. Actually, a woman these days who is a homemaker or a housewife is looked down on by many in our society.

Even the way women dress nowadays has changed. The Bible says in 1 Timothy 2:9 that God's women should dress in modest clothing. You see women in the church that dress just like the women in the world, who don't know God. They put on a mask of makeup, wear tight and revealing tops showing cleavage, and even wear short shorts and tight pants, showing off their butts. God's women should be holy and set apart, not only acting but looking different from the women of the world. There is very little holiness being taught in the American churches today.

In regards to the feminist agenda, my opinion is this. Many years ago, the devil started to push this idea that women can and should do the same things that men are doing. I believe that this opened the door for the Jezebel spirit to invade America. The Bible teaches that this spirit is a dominating and controlling demon that influences people, both men and women. This spirit has caused lots of women to usurp men's authority. Now many men in this country have been emasculated, hence a rise in homosexual men. Just because women can do the same things as men, doesn't mean that they should. Women got tricked into trying to prove this idea and started pursuing different careers and now they even fight in wars. I'm not saying that women don't have a right to do these things, but just understand that the devil is behind a lot of it. There is so much competition now between men and women and even husbands and wives over careers.

A hundred years ago when this country had more Christian values, women going to work was a rare thing. The devil then devised things like wars and inflation to make the prices of everything go up so much. Couples couldn't afford for the wife not to work anymore. All of this, just to get husbands and wives away from each other and their children. The old divide and conquer trick. He then sends his demons to work through other people at their jobs, to try to hit on them, and steer them away from their spouse. If not that, he gets them so focused on their job, that their family becomes second. The children are sent to school all day and then after school sports. Before you know it, the family spends so little time with each other that they grow apart. Husbands and wives start arguing all the time and children start rebelling against their parents. Eventually they only want to hang out with their friends. This is happening in so many families across America, even Christian ones.

We must realize that the Devil's plan is to split people up and eventually break them up. People wonder why the divorce rate in America is fifty percent, even in the church. It's because the devil wants to destroy everything God created. God says marriage is between a man and a woman. Now the devil makes man pass a law that men can marry men and women can marry women. The Bible says in Leviticus 20:13 that homosexuality is an abomination to the Lord. God makes man and the devil passes a law legalizing abortion to justify killing man. The Bible says in Exodus 20:13 that killing is a sin and abortion is murder. We must wake people up to what the enemy is doing to our society before it's too late.

I believe that if we go back to following Biblical principles in this country. A lot of these plans of the enemy would be exposed and maybe things could turn around in America. A good start would be if women actually submitted to their husbands in everything and husbands actually loved their wives as the Bible says in Ephesians 5:22-25. The family unit would be a lot stronger and there would be a lot less divorce in this country. What about Christians opening family businesses so that their families spend more time together. Like in the old days, most people had their own farms or businesses and parents actually homeschooled their children. Let's stop putting all the responsibility on the world system to support us, feed us, and educate us. I went off on a tangent, but I believe this had to be said.

Anyways getting back to my story, this situation with Grace added to my depression. Even though I had forgiven her, and she had forgiven me. The devil used this to get me to go wild in the clubs. I did begin spending more time with her, and our relationship got stronger. I even started taking her out with me to the clubs a lot. At the same time, I started sleeping around with women and didn't care about the consequences. Before this I was kind of reserved and careful about what I did because I did not want to get caught but now, I felt free and went crazy.

My main place to party for years was the Hard Rock Hotel and Casino because they had a few different clubs there. It was close to my house in Broward County. I was a regular there, and became a VIP at the biggest club there, which was called Spirits back then. The name says it all because I was being influenced by a lot of demonic spirits. VIP is a big deal in the club world, and I thought I was the man. So, then I started to frequent other popular nightclubs in the Miami area. Little did I know that things in Miami were different than I had experienced before. Especially in South Beach, where going to hottest parties, meant you were somebody and you had money.

Miami is the place where all the entertainment industry people and ballers from all over the U.S and even the world went to have fun. It is often called the playboys paradise because the most beautiful and exotic women from all over the world go there. I quickly fell in love with the South Beach scene. I had been partying in Miami for many years but sporadically. When I started becoming a regular out there was when I realized that it was really a hangout for the rich and famous.

The problem was, I was not rich nor was I famous, but I still wanted to hang out there. I just loved to party and being around the who's who in music, sports, and entertainment was normal for me. I had been doing it ever since I went to Cancun with my brother at eighteen years old and I wanted to continue. I don't know why, but I just felt comfortable being around stars. Ever since I was eighteen, something inside of me, would tell me that I was meant for something great. Being empty and depressed, I was still searching for what that something was. I know now that what I was searching for was God and to find my purpose and calling in life.

After some time of partying in Miami, I started to get a lot of negative attention. The club promoters and DJs controlled the party scene, and I was not really cool with them. One, because I was not rich or famous and second, because I knew something was off with them. At one point I even started getting offers to start promoting parties in my area. Who knows, if I had done it, maybe today I would be some big famous DJ or promoter. Fortunately, I turned those people down because I noticed a lot of darkness around the whole nightclub scene.

At this time, I was learning a lot about the Illuminati and secret societies from my conversations with Dave and research online. I believe the devil wanted to get me so depressed and desperate for money and fame. That I would sell my soul and officially join these DJs and promoters, who I believe, were working for the forces of darkness.

You see I always had a way with people in the club world. Men respected me, some even looked up to me, and women were attracted to me. I used to think that it was the New York swagger that girls would tell me that I had. I came to find out later that it was a gift that God had given me to be able to influence people. The thing is, God gives all of us gifts. The question is, are we using the gifts for God's Kingdom or the devil's? I was never really an outgoing person, but I always knew that I was different, and people could see it. I believe the enemy wanted to use me in the party world to lure countless more men and women into that destructive way of life. Basically, he wanted me to sign a contract with him and win souls for him full time. Thank God that he opened my eyes and saved me before it was too late.

Ephesians 6:12 "For we wrestle not against flesh and blood, but against principalities, against powers, against the rulers of the darkness of this world, against spiritual wickedness in high places."

After turning the devil down, I started to have a lot of demonic attacks. I would have guys staring me down and trying to intimidate me when I went out. If I wasn't going to join them, they didn't want me coming to their parties anymore and I knew it. With me being used to confrontation and really not caring about anything anymore, I still went. I didn't know it at the time, but God was using all of this to turn me into a soldier and to remove the fear of man from my life. At one point it got so bad that I had people parked in front of my house watching me and my family for weeks.

I even started to get death threats. I had girls call me and tell me that some guys were going to kill me. One night I came out of a club at like 5am and when I got to my car, there was something that looked like a black flag laying on the hood of my car. Our BMW had gotten repossessed one night while Grace and I were on South Beach partying. What an embarrassing experience that was. So, I was now driving a white Audi convertible and this black flag was hard to miss. No one said anything to me that night, but I believe that someone was warning me, that they were serious and getting ready to take me out. I had heard gangsters talk about this kind of thing, so I knew that this meant something bad.

Nevertheless, I kept hearing a voice in my head telling me to just get high and go out to the clubs anyway. I know now that it was the devil and his demons trying everything, they could to destroy me. I have forgiven all of those people who were coming against me back then and pray for them because they did not really know what they were doing. They were just being used by the devil, who had been trying to destroy me ever since the day I was born. Soon after, I started to hear these voices(demons) tell me to kill myself. I eventually became suicidal, and it got so bad that I even contemplated killing my wife and my children also. I actually went out one day and bought a gun and was going to do it.

This all came to a breaking point when, one day after years of complaining to her. My mother felt sorry for me and agreed to have us come to NY. I had been telling her for a long time that I was depressed and wanted to do something new like open a business. The law firms and loan modification companies that I previously worked for had closed down. Some of them came under investigation because they were defrauding people, taking their money and not helping them. I could not trust these businesses anymore, so I wanted to start my own loan modification business. The problem was that after all the fraud a law was passed that you had to be affiliated with a law firm to do that. With my mom being a lawyer, I had been trying to get her to help me do it for years, but she wouldn't. This is when she finally agreed to it.

Little did I know it was God's plan of escape for me and his timing was perfect. I had become fearful for my life and was so close to being destroyed by the enemy. By this time, it started to become very clear to me that the devil was real. My eyes were being opened and God was starting to draw me to himself.

One of the last times I went to a club in South Florida. I was in the club, and I heard the DJ say more than once: If anyone believes in God put your hands in the air. I immediately threw my hand in the air as I wondered to myself why was he asking this? I had never remembered ever hearing a DJ ask this before. The shocking thing to me was that, among the hundreds of people that were there. I was one of, if not the only one with my hand in the air. It was like a confirmation for me that most of these people were not of God but were of the devil and they knew it. I was not saved at the time and I lived a very worldly life, but I did believe in God. I just didn't know that believing in God meant you must read and obey his word, the Bible.

CHAPTER 8
SALVATION GRACE COMES TO MY FAMILY

Romans 2:4 "Or despisest thou the riches of his goodness and forbearance and longsuffering; not knowing that the goodness of God leadeth thee to repentance?"

In early 2013, I took my family to NY, and we stayed with my mother in her two-bedroom apartment. Shortly after going there, I got another confirmation. My wife and I went out to a nightclub one night and it happened again. This time I had Grace there as a witness, so I was not going crazy. The DJ said in the middle of the music blasting: If anyone believes in God put your hands in the air. Grace and I looked at each other and excitedly threw our hands up. As we looked around, we saw that no one but us had their hands up. We then knew that God was showing us that nightclubs are not the place where God's people should be. If I remember correctly, that was my last time ever going to a nightclub.

After that night, in April, right around my son Amani's birthday, we noticed something white in his left eye. We immediately took him to the hospital and soon after found out that he had a tumor inside his eye. The growth of the tumor caused him to develop a cataract. That was the white thing we saw, that got our attention and made us bring him in. God is amazing because the doctors said that if he had never gotten that cataract. The tumor could have grown into his head without us knowing and eventually killed him. After lots of examinations and doctors talking with other doctors about him. They diagnosed Amani with a very rare form of cancer, called a medulloepithelioma. It only happens in like one out of a half of a million children.

You can imagine us finding this out after going through all that chaos we had been going through. I was a mess and I really could have given up after this, but somehow I felt God's hand on us. One afternoon after coming from the eye hospital in New York City, which had one of the best doctors in the country for my son's situation. I ran into my cousin David at a health food store in Long Island, near my mom's apartment. When I told him about my son's situation, he told me not to do it.

We had just that day decided to schedule him for surgery to remove his eye. We had been going back and forth to that doctor for almost a month. They had been checking the rate of growth in the tumor every week to see how aggressive it was. When they saw that it was growing every week, they told us that we should remove the eye, therefore removing the tumor. We really didn't want to do it, but they told us that if we didn't, he could die. The doctors were so nonchalant about taking out a child's eye, it was scary. They told us when he got a little older, he could just put in a fake eye. It didn't feel right to us, but we were scared and agreed to do it.

God used my cousin that day to tell us to put Amani on a fast which we immediately did. He went on a thirty-day vegetable only fast, along with taking some other products that we got him. To our amazement when we took him back to the doctor a month later. The tumor had stopped growing and it has not grown at all since. Glory to God!

During these months I was doing a lot of research in books and online about all the things that were being put in our food. I learned that the GMOs, the chemicals, the sugars, the salts, and all the toxins were destroying our bodies. I stayed up many nights for months into the early hours of the morning researching different things. I had no idea what we were doing to ourselves by eating fast food all the time. I had been feeding my children nothing but junk food for years, because I did not know any better.

Since I was a young teenager and my parents were always working, I used to eat a lot of McDonald's and Burger King myself. They were the closest fast-food places to my house in West Hempstead. As I grew older and was able to drive, I began eating Wendy's, Dunkin Donuts, and White Castle, which was my after the club favorite because it was open 24hrs. Over the years I got hooked on fast food and eating in restaurants especially when I lived on my own. I wasn't really into cooking, so I ate in the streets for most of my life. Even after Grace and I started living together, we would cook sometimes, but most of the time we ate out or ordered pizza or Chinese food. When we moved to Florida we were constantly in different restaurants and that was just a part of our lifestyle.

As I got into my 30s, I think my bad eating habits started to take a toll on my body. I would get tired a lot, and I would end up taking naps throughout the day. I would also get moody a lot and I know now that part of it had to do with my poor eating habits. When my son got sick, I studied the effects of GMOs (genetically modified organisms), pesticides, and toxins. A lot of the processed foods in our grocery stores today are full of these things. So, when I found out that big companies were purposely putting these things into the food to dumb down the population and make us sick. We changed our diets and began eating only organic and non-gmo foods. We actually became ninety percent vegan, eating fish on occasion, for a couple of years.

Surprisingly, once we changed our diet and started detoxing our bodies. We each lost between twenty-five and thirty-five pounds. As we lost the weight and got rid of all that junk in our brains and bodies, we even started to think more clearly. It was like a night and day difference from how we used to see things. We started to become more aware of other crazy things that were going on around us and how much of a stronghold the enemy really had on society. I really believe that food is one of the enemy's most effective weapons. Against the people in the world and against the people of God because most of them don't know what's happening to them.

Hosea 4:6 "My people are destroyed for lack of knowledge."

Once I had overcome the attack on Amani's health and then on my own body. All the other struggles that I had been dealing with, became so small. I had awoken to the fact that nothing was more important than my family and our health. Then ultimately, I came to realize that even more important than those things was my family's salvation.

Ephesians 2:8 "For by grace are ye saved through faith; and that not of yourselves: it is the gift of God"

In the middle of all the chaos I was going through, God stepped in and delivered my family and I from all of it. He had been drawing us to himself for some time but on November 7, 2013 Grace, Amani (11 years old at the time), Sanai(9 years old), and I all gave our lives to Jesus Christ. We were sitting on our couch watching a Billy Graham show on TV called My Hope America. We had moved back to our house in South Florida a couple of months prior to this, but it was the greatest and most important day of our lives. By the grace of God, we repented of all our sins. We gave ourselves one hundred percent to the Lord Jesus Christ and asked him to fill us with the Holy Spirit.

What a glorious day it was! Coming to know and experience God's love for the first time. Words cannot explain how it feels to know the God of the universe, the one that created you, and loves you. Being filled with the Holy

Spirit and having that personal experience with the Father is the only thing that really matters in this life. Before that I was lost and in the worst danger that exists in the universe. Dying and going to hell is worse than any other thing that could happen to us on this earth.

Phillipians 4:8 "Finally, brethren, whatsoever things are true, whatsoever things are honest, whatsoever things are just, whatsoever things are pure, whatsoever things are lovely, whatsoever things are of good report; if there be any virtue, and if there be any praise, think on these things."

Soon after our radical encounter, Jesus started to set me and my family free from our addictions to smoking weed, alcohol, pornography, worldly hip hop/rap music, worldly tv shows, and fast food. By the grace of God, I was no longer what the Bible calls, "a whoremonger". I also, since that time, never even thought about going to a nightclub again. Which is also a big miracle, in itself.

Almost immediately after getting saved my wife and I, by his grace, were delivered from those things that this world had had us in bondage to. We had become new creatures in Christ!

2 Corinthians 5:17 "Therefore if any man be in Christ, he is a new creature: old things are passed away; behold, all things are become new."

CHAPTER 9
WALKING WITH JESUS

Many people believe that when they get born again and surrender to Jesus Christ, that their life will just become easy. The truth is, that the devil will probably attack you more once you get saved because he doesn't want you to fulfill your destiny. The difference is, that once you have salvation. God gives you the grace and the strength to go through the trials, so you are not alone. He is with you as the Holy Spirit lives in you, so you can have perfect peace in the middle of every storm. Once you know that you have passed from death unto life by being born again, you already have the victory! Thank God for Jesus, who said:

Matthew 11:30 "For my yoke is easy, and my burden is light."

Shortly after giving our lives to Christ, my family and I started reading the Bible and praying daily. Like I said God did a quick work, delivering us from a lot of things. Then we started going out and doing what the Bible says to do. We started talking to everyone we knew about Jesus and salvation. The funny thing is, that as we started to share our experience and minister to family and friends. We started to realize that most of them were not ready to hear what we had to say to them. Some of them thought that we had lost our minds.

We quickly came to find out that the gospel isn't for everyone. Meaning Jesus did die for the sins of the whole world, but only those who believe in, and obey him will have eternal life. What we learned is that most of our family and friends did believe in Jesus. The thing is, they did not want to obey his teachings/commandments, at least not yet anyway.

Our first I would say year of being saved was great but also very discouraging for us. On one hand, we were praying and reading our Bibles like crazy. We were really getting to know our heavenly Father which was amazing. On the other hand, we were saddened to learn that the truths about God that we were learning and sharing with others, were not widely accepted. In fact, none of our family members when we shared the gospel with them, wanted to get saved. They actually would say that they are already saved. We knew though, that by the way they lived, they were not yet born again and filled with God's Holy Spirit.

We knew that they had not yet had a real encounter with the Lord because when you truly encounter Him, your life completely changes. You cannot stay the same. When you start renewing your mind with the word of God, you begin to see things differently. You see through the eyes of Christ as you now have his mind. You start to hate and abhor sin and feel a burden to save those around you, who are lost. It is an unexplainable feeling, but I believe most believers once they really meet the Lord experience this.

Philippians 2:5 "Let this mind be in you which was also in Christ Jesus."

So we spent a good year, trying our best to minister to all of the people from our life before Christ, with little success. Until 2015 we had what seemed to be a breakthrough. Andrew, the best man at our wedding and childhood friend, called me from Dallas, Texas and wanted to receive Christ. We had been ministering to him and his wife for a while and they were finally ready to get saved.

The crazy thing about this was that, a couple of weeks before he called me. I met a brother named Oscar, who was about 20 years older than me, at the Wholefoods near our house in Miramar. He gave me a prophetic word, that he said that God told him to give me. Which was, that if I cut my hair off, God would bless me. At that time, I had long dreads that I had been growing for more than 12 years. I loved my hair, but I loved Jesus more. So the day he gave me that word, I went home and told Grace to cut it all off. Yup, I went from a head full of hair, to being bald. It was a drastic change, but I can tell you I felt so free when I did it. I obeyed the Lord, and then soon after I got this call from Andrew. He decided to fly our whole family out to Dallas, so that we could minister to and fellowship with his family. Glory to God!

We originally were only supposed to stay for about a week, but we ended up being there for about a month. Then we came home to Florida for a week and then went back out there. A little while after we got back to Dallas, I ended up being offered a youth Pastor position. It was at a church that we found there to get their family planted in. Little did we know it was a set up. God took us to that church and opened the door for us to stay there for a while. The Holy Ghost had us in school, teaching us. He wanted us to learn what to do, and what not to do, when we started our own ministry. Unfortunately, after doing that for a couple of months, my family and I were asked to leave that church. We were trying to tell one of the members about the dark times, that God was showing us was coming. To our surprise, the Pastor did not agree and told us not to scare "his people," and kicked us out. Shortly after this we came back to Florida from Dallas. Little did we know that we would start our own ministry.

The Lord called to start Warriors 4 Christ Ministries in April of 2015. We started a House Church in our home and started having fellowships in May. We also started officially doing street ministry with Jesus tshirts, signs, Bible tracts, and a megaphone. When you read the Bible, this is a big part of what Jesus and the Apostles did. They preached the Gospel in the streets. So Oscar, the brother I had met a few months prior, and I were on fire to start doing it. We started going to places that I used to frequent like the South Beach scene. We would use the megaphone and preach the gospel, which many people out there didn't like. We also started evangelizing at professional sports games and concerts.

It still amazes me, how the Lord delivered me from the bar and nightclub scene to clean me up and send me back to that scene to win the lost (those who don't know Jesus). God has now used me to give my testimony and minister to countless people who love the nightlife scene and by his grace we have seen many souls saved. A lot of people, even in ministry, think we are crazy for what we do. By God's grace, we have continued to go out in the streets and evangelize. Don't get me wrong, it is definitely dangerous ministering out in the streets. At any moment someone could do something to you, if they didn't like what they heard. Thank God that he gave us the boldness to do it as the Bible says; that the righteous are as bold as a lion. God had been preparing me all of my life to be a warrior for his Kingdom and to not be scared of men, so I wasn't.

Sometimes we would just go out evangelizing and pass out tracts. We love using Bible tracts. They are a powerful way to share the gospel. They are easy to give to people if you can't have a conversation with them. Tracts are a little pamphlet with Bible scripture references and instructions for getting saved. Sometimes when we went out, we would meet other believers and would be able to encourage them. Many times though, it would be unbelievers and some would get saved. When they did, we invited them to our home fellowships that we did on Saturdays. We also started doing Bible studies on Wednesday evenings.

I was not really into social media and being online, but I felt like the Lord wanted me to start doing videos online. I first started on an App called Periscope and then went on

Facebook and YouTube. I ended up doing videos once or twice a week on Periscope for maybe a year or two. Sadly, that platform has been taken down now and I had nearly a hundred videos on there. I now have to figure out how to retrieve them all.

When I look back, I see how that one act of obedience (cutting my hair off), I believe opened the door for so many things to start happening in our lives.

Isaiah 1:19 "If ye be willing and obedient, ye shall eat the good of the land."

In 2016, the Lord called us to sell our home and move to McKinney, Texas. This was our next big test. Again, we loved our home, but we loved God more, so we did it. This was our dream home and had been in it for about 11 years. We didn't think we would ever move, but the Bible says obedience is better than sacrifice. You see, after being saved, we started getting dreams and visions of a mega tsunami coming to Florida and the East Coast. The Lord never told us when it was coming, but the more we got these dreams, the more urgency we felt. It was one of the things that gave us the push to leave Florida. One day, early in 2016, the Lord told us that we needed to put our house on the market for sale. We then went through a lot of warfare to sell our home.

The real estate market was pretty hot at the time. The first weekend that we put the house on the market, we got 2 offers. When that happened, we thought it was going to be a smooth process. Little did we know, it would take us about

6 months to actually get the house sold. It should have been a 2-to-3-month process, but there were all kinds of delays and setbacks. It got so bad, that even when we got to the closing table, we could not close because the funds disappeared. Almost 4 hundred thousand dollars, that was being transferred from the buyer's bank to our bank was stolen. Someone tried to steal the money and the FBI had to be called to investigate the matter.

A few days before the closing, the A/C unit in the house stopped working right in the middle of us packing up to move. The timing of it was crazy! It was the middle of the summer and very hot outside, so we could not stay in the house once we finished packing. Then when the money went missing. We didn't know what to do, so went into fasting, worship, and prayer to get God's help. Thank God that the money was eventually recovered. We were able to close and get the funds we needed to move to Texas.

CHAPTER 10
CALLED TO GREATNESS

Since being saved, God has had us at about seven or eight different churches, even while having our own ministry. At each church, we spent between six to nine months, learning and growing in our faith. The second church we went to, was a small prophetic church about 10 minutes away from our house in Florida. One day, at one of the services, something unexpected happened. The Pastor called me up to the front of the Church. He laid his hands on me and told me that God is sending me out as a Prophet to his people. I didn't know exactly what that meant at the time as I was just learning about the prophetic. Up to that point, the Lord was using me mainly as an Evangelist. I had a passion in me to win souls for Jesus, but this started to change, shortly after this experience. I started to have a burden to warn people about the things that the Lord was showing me.

God had been speaking to me about certain calamities that were coming for a while. So when we started our ministry the Lord began using me prophetically, also to give warnings to the church. Telling people and ministries in Florida that a tsunami was coming, was not easy. Many did not believe it and did not receive the word, but I continued to warn people. I believe that as the Lord saw that I was faithful to give the word to those people that he brought into my path. He then started giving me specific prophetic words/warnings for Church leaders and America.

As I was obedient to put out these warnings on our online platforms, we came under a lot of persecution. Especially from other believers, who did not want to believe the words. Many of them said, we were preaching doom and gloom and that I was too negative. Nevertheless, all glory to God, but many of the words we have given have come to pass or are coming to pass today. Life in America has totally changed in the last few years. Things have gotten progressively worse, as God has been warning us it would, through his Prophets for many years.

Amos 3:7 "Surely the Lord God will do nothing, but he revealeth his secret unto his servants the prophets."

When we got to Texas, the Lord blessed us with a nice 3 bedroom apartment in McKinney, Texas. The Holy Spirit had been highlighting that city to us, months before we even moved. He told us that he was calling us to McKinney. When we got here, we immediately bought 5,000 Bible tracts and started hitting the streets, passing them out and talking to people. As we started doing ministry here in Texas, we realized that people here were a lot more receptive to the gospel. Not only that but people were a lot more friendly and open. You see Texas is in the Bible Belt, where many people grew up hearing the gospel and going to church. So whereas probably 70-80 percent of people in South Florida would reject the Bible tracts we tried to give them. 70-80 percent of the people here in the North Dallas area actually take the tracts, which is a huge difference.

In 2017 the Lord brought us into a wilderness season where we became homeless. We had been trusting him for our provision and he had been providing for us every day since being saved. We were mainly doing full time ministry and living by faith. Grace was homeschooling our children and did not work. I didn't have a full time job, but I did drive for Uber sometimes. I did that, really just to minister to people as it could not pay all of our bills. Jesus burned this scripture into my heart and mind so that I had the faith to believe him to pay our bills and he did.

Matthew 6:33 "But seek ye first the kingdom of God, and his righteousness; and all these things shall be added unto you."

In the summer of that year though, the donations and help we had been receiving, dried up and we had to leave our apartment. We were believing for God to supernaturally get us a house when we left that apartment. Little did we know that we were going to be without our own home for the next 2 years. At one point we even lost the Cadillac suv that someone had blessed us with shortly after getting saved. Now, we actually had no car and had to borrow a friend of the family's vehicle to get around.

This time of us being homeless was one of the toughest periods of our lives, but Jesus was with us every step of the way. Looking back on it, we really learned to trust God on a deeper level and our faith grew so strong during this time. We were living on food stamps, so we never starved and whenever we needed something people would help us out. We even had other homeless people buy us food and we knew that it was God using them.

We slept in our car sometimes for 5 days straight with no shower, until someone would get us a hotel room for a day or a week. It was definitely a humbling experience, for us to have to ask everyone we knew or met for help, just to have a bed to sleep in. Our family had always had everything we needed and didn't know what it was to be without. I believe the Lord allowed us to experience this season, to humble us and teach us to be content no matter what we have or don't have. God teaches us this through Apostle Paul in the Bible.

Philippians 4:11-12 "For I have learned, in whatsoever state I am, therewith to be content. I know both how to be abased, and I know how to abound."

In 2018, after fasting, praying, and crying out to the Lord many times. The family friend named Patrick that let us use his car, offered to let us stay in his house. The only catch was that it was back in Florida. We had spent about a year going from hotel to hotel and sleeping in our car, all while still evangelizing in the streets of North Dallas. I had been trying to get a job and even applied at Walmart a couple of times, but no one would even call me back. So after praying about it, we knew it was part of God's plan, so we went back to Florida. It was actually a blessing because Patrick had a beautiful vacation home in the Orlando area. He did not live there, so we basically had the house all to ourselves most of the time.

While we were in Florida, God ended up using us to warn a lot of people and ministries again about the calamities that were coming. He sent us from the north to the south and from the east to the west coast of Florida. If you have never been there, Florida is a huge state, so we did a lot of driving. The funny thing is, this time many of the people and even Pastors we spoke with. Were actually prepared and received the words/warnings that we gave them. Literally dozens of people that we met during that year actually had had similar dreams/visions or words from God about a coming tsunami, chaos, and destruction.

We were also doing a lot of praying and fasting during this time so that may have had something to do with it. Not that we didn't pray before and we had learned early in our walk about living a lifestyle of fasting, but we really made them our focus now. In 2018 while at his house I also took a course to become a claims adjuster and I got my Texas Claims Adjuster license.

So we stayed in Patrick's house for about a year, until one day the Lord told us to go back to Dallas. We were hesitant at first because we didn't want to have to go back to hopping around from hotel to hotel, but we were obedient. In late 2019 when we got back to Texas, God opened the door for us to rent a beautiful 1 year old, 4-bedroom, 4 bathroom, 2900 sq foot house in McKinney.

The way that we know it was the will of God was because we had bad credit and no job, so only he could get us a home. We almost got evicted from that first apartment we had, so no one would rent to us. Miraculously these homeowners approved us to rent their home, after we were turned down by countless others.

By the grace of God we were also able to get a car of our own that year. The Lord blessed us with a 2016 white Infiniti SUV which was also a miracle, considering our credit was poor. A word that the Holy Spirit gave me when we moved back to McKinney was; He wanted me to serve the community. So we now had a roof over our head and an suv that I could do Uber with.

Driving people around and ministering to their needs through Uber, was what I was called to do at that time, so I immediately did it. Shortly after moving into our new home God told me that he sent me to the Dallas area as an Apostle and wanted me to start a church here. God had spoken to me years prior that he was calling me to be an Apostle, but I didn't know when it would happen. He now confirmed this was the time through multiple ways. One of which was, one day after not talking to Oscar (who was like a mentor to me) for maybe 6 months, he called me out of the blue and told me that I am an Apostle. I was shocked, but I knew it was God because I had been praying for confirmation before I started calling myself that.

Matthew 23:11 Jesus said: "But he that is greatest among you shall be your servant."

So in 2019, we started our home church in McKinney, Texas. We had services in our home on Saturday afternoons and Bible studies on Wednesdays evenings. It grew pretty quickly as we were meeting a lot of people, being out in the streets all the time. Once we started having more than 20 people in our home, we started to get overwhelmed. Especially with me working, our family growing, and having to maintain our own relationship with God, it was a lot. At that time, we were pregnant with our youngest son, Josiah and we had 2 more children, Noah who was born in 2014 and Hannah who was born in 2017. God was definitely multiplying us and blessing us in every area of our lives and we were grateful.

In 2020, the pandemic happened, and our street ministry kind of slowed down as people were not really going out. God had told us that the pandemic was coming back in 2019 through a supernatural encounter with a Prophetess we were connected to. The Lord had us put out warnings about the coming pandemic on the streets and on Facebook starting in April 2019, so we were not surprised when it hit in January 2020. Then even after the lockdowns, we were still having our services on Saturdays and Bible studies on Wednesdays. Everything was good for a while, but things started to change towards the end of 2020.

We believe, due to all of the uncertainty during the pandemic. Our landlords decided to move back to Texas and wanted their home back. Once again, we went through a lot of warfare during this time. We searched for months, but could not find another home to rent and were turned down by everyone. Landlords were just too scared to rent their homes to just anyone during this period, so we ended up getting evicted from the house. We had been paying the rent every month just fine, but when the pandemic came. It really messed everything up for the Landlords, so they had to move back into their house.

Again, by God's grace and mercy, we were able to find another house to rent. Patrick had to help us this time, but we literally got approved for another house a couple days before we were supposed to be evicted. This is after trying for quite a few other houses, but this is the door that finally opened. The funny thing is, this house was an older house but it was a lot bigger than the one we were in. It was a 5-bedroom 3-bathroom home in Mckinney, at almost 3500 sq feet. We did not expect to rent such a big home, but God put us in it. Our God is a provider, and his ways are higher than our ways!!

In 2021 the Lord blessed me with a claims adjuster job that I could work from home. I had been trying to get a claims job since getting the license, but the door finally opened in August 2021. It was a contract job so there were no benefits but the pay was really good, at almost six figures. That lasted about 7 months. I was working ten hours a day, six days a week, slaving until God called me to quit. He wanted me to start working more on ministry and the transportation business that he called me to start during the pandemic. In 2020-21 Uber was very slow due to the pandemic, so I started doing private rides for people. God had called me to start a transportation business like Uber, but Christian. In 2023 is when it became official, as I incorporated it, got my business cards done, and set up a website.

I believe that God called me to start this business to employ believers in these last days. The pandemic showed us that we cannot trust the world system to employ us during tough times. Also, the world is moving to a cashless system and the Bible says that one day. We will not be able to buy or sell unless we take the mark of the beast (the devil) in your right hand or your forehead. This could be the implantable microchip that is being promoted all over the world right now. The Bible says that anyone who takes the mark, cannot go to heaven. So we Christians will have to have our own businesses and finances in these last days to survive. We have to go back to the way things used to be.

In 2021 Jesus also called me to start The Church of Dallas, a fellowship for training and equipping Saints to do the work of the ministry and endure during these end times. Jesus said go and make disciples, so that is what we are doing. The Lord led us to a building in downtown McKinney, where we rented a room and had our first meeting in December. By the grace of God, we are now doing weekly Bible studies in our home and on Zoom on Wednesday evenings. Also, we have weekly Saturday afternoon services in a hotel here and the ministry is growing. In July 2022, we started a Zoom prayer call that we do on Tuesday and Thursday evenings as well.

On March 11, 2023, I was ordained as an Apostle, pastoring the Church of Dallas at Mckinney. Bishop Antonio, who has been in ministry for almost 40 years and who I had known for 8 years. Is the one who God used to ordain me on earth. Even though I was already ordained by God. Interestingly enough, I met him right before the Lord called us to start Warriors 4 Christ Ministries 8 years prior. So it made sense when he called me one day and told me that he wanted to ordain and endorse me as an Apostle for ministry. He had watched my family and I grow over the years and was there with us through the ups and downs of our time in ministry. The Bible says that God is the one who gives these gifts or positions to men, but he uses men to confirm or endorse you on earth.

Ephesians 4:11 "And he gave some, apostles; and some, prophets; and some, evangelists; and some, pastors and teachers."

As an Apostle, by God's grace and strength, I continue to serve and obey him. Even though, it has not been easy and our family goes through a lot of warfare. Despite all the trials and tribulations, God has been moving in our midst. Grace and I now have 5 children and just celebrated our 29th anniversary. We have been married for over 19 years and have never been more in love. Our family is living a victorious life, on fire for Jesus Christ and preaching his word all over the streets and airways of America. We give our Lord and Savior Jesus Christ all the glory, honor, and praise for what he is doing in us and through us! We can do nothing without him!!

Romans 8:31 "What shall we say about such wonderful things as these? If God is for us, who can ever be against us?"

IF HE DID IT FOR US, HE CAN DO IT FOR YOU TOO!!!

THE END

If you would like more information about us or you would like to support the work that Jesus has called us to do, here is our info:

Warriors 4 Christ Ministries

P.O Box 2077 McKinney TX 75070

Warriors4christministries.net